Pandemic Poetry
Across the Fence

Robinne Weiss

Global Pandemic

Late in 2019, a novel virus appeared in Wuhan, China. Covid-19, as the respiratory disease caused by the virus came to be called, quickly spread throughout the world. On 28 February 2020, New Zealand recorded its first case. On 11 March, the World Health Organisation officially declared Covid-19 a pandemic.

Governments around the world began restricting people's movements in order to stem the spread of the virus. In New Zealand, by mid-March, anyone arriving from overseas was required to self-isolate for 14 days, and the border was closed to anyone except citizens and permanent residents. Indoor gatherings of more than 100 people were cancelled. Overseas, governments were placing their citizens in lockdowns as cases of Covid-19 ballooned, overwhelming medical services.

On 21 March, Prime Minister Jacinda Ardern announced a four-level alert system for Covid-19. Each level, from one to four was more restrictive than the previous. At the same time, she announced we were at level two.

On 23 March, Ms Ardern announced we were moving to alert level three immediately, and would transition to level four in 48 hours. The nation scrambled to prepare for a lockdown in which only essential services—the food supply chain and medical services—were allowed to operate.

The Poems

The day before lockdown, my husband and I sold our house. The new house was still being built, so the family moved into the shed on the new property. We began lockdown in a new community, living in cramped, cold quarters.

I started my pandemic poems—written with a Sharpie on scraps of building wrap and posted on the fence out front—to keep myself sane during lockdown and connect with the new neighbours I'd never met. Forty-nine days, forty-nine poems.

I wanted them to be positive, but some days I wrote half a dozen poems and rejected every one because they were dark reflections of my mood. I kept writing, however, until I found the light of good thoughts.

And by forcing myself to focus on the positive, I began to feel it.

The neighbours must have felt it too. They stopped and read the poems silently to themselves. They read them aloud to their children. They laughed. They came by every day to read the next instalment.

And I listened to them from the shed and smiled.

The day after I took them all down, symbolically freeing us from lockdown, I found a lovely note pinned to the gate: Thank you for your amazing efforts along your fence. You brightened our days...

Which, of course, was the whole point.

Day 1
26 March

The first day of lockdown was eerily quiet. No one knew quite what to do. Normal life had suddenly stopped, and we were still wondering how we were going to fill our days.

Day 2
27 March

The odd stillness of lockdown was compounded by the first good rain in months. We were holed up, but the shape of our lockdown was yet to form.

Day 3
28 March

We fell into a routine of walks—morning, noon, evening—three a day, weather permitting. It was the only way we were allowed out.

Day 4
29 March

Our first rain in months had now been falling for four days. Plants responded by greening up after a hot dry summer had turned them brown. The life seemed to defy the increasingly dire news from around the world as the coronavirus took hold.

Day 5
30 March

In a nation of outdoorsy people on forced holiday, many wanted to go surfing, tramping and mountain biking. But in addition to breaking the virus transmission cycle, lockdown was supposed to free our medical system for the possible influx of thousands of sick people. We weren't allowed to do risky things, for fear of taxing those at the front lines of the virus response.

Day 6
31 March

Houses are our space ships.
Astronauts all,
We set our coordinates
For a distant planet,
Travel through time and space,
And step out into a new world.

By the end of our first week of lockdown, it was clear the world was changing rapidly. Life as we knew it was over, maybe forever.

Day 7
1 April

Dogs seemed to love lockdown—their beloved families were home all the time and going for walks multiple times a day. Cats appeared less impressed. We got the distinct impression ours wanted more personal space.

Day 8
2 April

Social media was alight with people noticing grey roots and wondering how long it would be before they could get their hair dyed again. I have always embraced my own grey hair, but I thought that at this time showing grey roots was a mark of survivorship.

Day 9
3 April

Walking past lighted houses in the evenings occasionally felt like being inside a Norman Rockwell painting—families sitting around the kitchen table in pools of golden light sharing a meal or playing a board game. Of course, not everyone had a safe family life to shelter in, but the warmth of the family circle was important for many.

Day 10
4 April

Hurray for the weekend!
It's time to go out.
Get dressed in your best.
You'll have fun, there's no doubt.

But wait! What is this?
The pubs are all shut.
The restaurants, the clubs—
We're all stuck in a rut.

I suppose we'll just have to
Go out for a walk,
Or stay home and play Scrabble,
Or use FaceTime to talk
To friends who, right now
Seem so far away.
But don't worry,
We'll get there,
We'll be through this someday.

Even homebodies were beginning to feel constrained and hemmed in. In our household, the daily joke over breakfast was to ask what everyone was going to do for the day. The stock answer was, "I think I'll stay home. Maybe go for a walk later. Then ... I don't know ... maybe I'll stay home some more."

Day 11
5 April

Our hand basin,
Who art in the bathroom,
Hallowed be thy tap.
Thy hand soap run.
Thy germs be gone
From hands and under
    fingernails.
Give us this day our daily scrub
And forgive us for hoarding
    hand sanitiser
As we forgive those who cleaned
    out the toilet paper.
Lead us not to hoard wine,
But deliver us some nice fruits
    and vegetables.
For thine is the germ-busting
    power of soap
For ever and ever.
Amen.

Public service messages were frequent and clear—stay home, wash your hands, shop normally when you go for groceries. Here in New Zealand, product shortages were minor and generally short-lived, but the ongoing hoarding and shortages of grocery items overseas was a source of wonderment—exactly what were Americans doing with all that toilet paper?

Day 12
6 April

The human world felt unsafe, so many of us retreated to the natural world. We weren't allowed to travel to our favourite wild places, but our slower-paced life allowed us time to note the wild beauty of our own back yards.

Day 13
7 April

Autumn sun glows warm
On a face lifted skyward,
Eyes closed to the cold.

We turned our focus inward to our immediate neighbours, our family, our homes. We could only watch the rest of the world in horror, but we could do concrete things to keep the people in our bubbles happy and safe. It was small solace, but it was solace.

Day 14
8 April

We were blessed in New Zealand to have a prime minister who led with strength and compassion. We were locked down under some of the stricter rules in the world, but Jacinda made sure we were all taken care of, even the children. She not only gave a briefing specifically for kids, but as Easter loomed, she made certain to assure children that the Easter Bunny was an essential service.

The tooth fairy's coming, it's true
She's an essential service for you.
So eat pretzels and candy,
It's all fine and dandy
When old teeth make way for the new.

The tooth fairy was also among the essential services Jacinda assured children would still be running during lockdown. Of course, if parents had no gold coins at home, the tooth fairy would have to get creative, because cash was difficult to come by.

Day 16
10 April

Because schools were shut during level four, the Ministry of Education moved the autumn school holidays forward to coincide with the first two weeks of lockdown. It was the strangest school holiday ever. Family vacations were replaced by neighbourhood strolls. People put teddy bears in their windows to create a sort of teddy bear scavenger hunt for bored children.

Day 17
11 April

We've got the lockdown blues,
The lockdown blues.
Ain't no point in even puttin' on shoes.

Can't go out,
Can't stay in,
Tired of hangin' out
With our kin.

Don't know the day,
Don't know the hour.
When was the last time I had a shower?

We're tired of devices,
Sick of our screens.
We're all so bored
We're moping like teens.

We've learnt to bake bread,
Knit and crochet.
A walk 'round the block
We do twice a day.

We've got the lockdown blues,
The lockdown blues.
Ain't no point in even puttin' on shoes.

Day 18
12 April

Teddy bears and paper eggs,
The Easter Bunny's been,
But the holiday's most treasured things
Must all come from within.

There were no in-person Easter services. Around the neighbourhood, children put Easter egg drawings in windows and drew Easter messages on the sidewalks with chalk.

Day 19
13 April

Days were getting shorter. Autumn was in the air. But the natural world seemed relatively unchanging compared to the human world. News from overseas became more and more dire, while here in New Zealand, it appeared our efforts were having a dramatic effect on the virus.

Day 20
14 April

Covid reveals what
The important things are—
Not shopping or travel
Or driving the car—
But the love of our whānau,
    neighbours and friends,
Kindness and humour.
So when this all ends
Let's never forget that what kept
    us going
Was the light of unity steadily
    glowing.

Life had changed dramatically. Sometimes we struggled to remember the time before Covid. There were things about our new life that were better than the old, and others that weren't. Here in New Zealand, there was a sense of shared purpose in our lockdown. As our case numbers improved, our collective resolve seemed to solidify.

Day 21
15 April

Children and teachers go back to school,
But it's not an ordinary day.
A video lesson, a shared Google doc.
Are the students all there? Who can say?
We muddle on through.
What else can we do?
While Covid-19 has its day.

School started up again, though not in person. The Ministry of Education and teachers around the country dove into distance education, learning by the seat of their pants how to deliver lessons online, on television, and through the post.

Day 22
16 April

Lock the door and throw out the key.
Covid-19 ain't gonna get me.

I've washed my hands twenty seconds for sure
'Cause it's a nasty disease without a cure.

I'm safe in my bubble with family and pets.
As lockdowns go, that's as good as it gets.

Movies and board games, tossing a ball.
We're all settled in for the long haul.

We knew we were doing well on the virus, but by mid-April, we were all tired of the unending sameness of lockdown. Keeping spirits up became more difficult.

Day 23
17 April

Around the world, lockdowns were providing space for nature to recover and return to urban areas. Sports fields grew lush, verges went unmowed, streets were quiet. I imagined New Zealand's mountains resting in the peace of our absence.

Day 24
18 April

I have thrown my watch away:
The magpie tells me when morning's
    arrived,
My stomach announces lunch.
It's time for tea when the water is hot,
And anytime's good for brunch.
Dinner we make as the sun's light
    fades,
And wine is for after dark.
Bedtime is sometime when boredom
    takes hold
And exhaustion puts out our spark.

Daily routines slowed down and relied less on the clock and more on our bodies' needs. There were late nights, early mornings, late mornings, and early nights. Meals happened when someone expressed hunger. Chocolate was consumed at all hours.

Day 25
19 April

Creativity blossomed during lockdown, with people finding new ways to reach out to one another every day. In some ways, confining us to boxes freed us to think outside them.

What is most important?
He tāngata
who care for our tamariki.
He tāngata
who care for our sick.
He tāngata
who ensure we are fed.
He tāngata
who lead.
He tāngata
who follow.
He tāngata.
He tāngata.
He tāngata.

The economy was at a virtual standstill in order to snuff out the virus. But it was clear from our government's response that the economy was not its first concern. He aha te mea nui o te ao? He tāngata, he tāngata, he tāngata. What is the most important thing in the world? The people, the people, the people.

The storm rages 'round us
We're soaked to the skin
Our ship pitched and tossed in the waves.
The captain barks orders,
Hand firm on the wheel.
She knows the relief her crew craves.

But she cannot allow us
Our petty desires,
As much as she longs for them too.
To weather the storm
We must all pull together
Or the tempest takes many, not few.

Lockdown was extended at least two more weeks. But we were alive, and cases of Covid-19 were dwindling. We could see our efforts were making a difference.

Day 28
22 April

There once was a country down under
That watched the others all blunder.
They looked at the facts,
Said, "We must all act!"
And ripped that poor virus asunder.

The international news kept us on our course, in spite of our growing desire to go out. It was clear that we had done something amazing here—something few other countries had managed. If we could stay the course, we might just beat this virus without the massive death toll other nations were suffering.

Day 29
23 April

Having come to the point I'd expected to stop writing daily poems, only to have lockdown extended was a bit of a struggle. How could I keep my own spirits up enough to continue to produce positive, funny, or uplifting poems every day? I wasn't sure how I would do it, but stopping was not an option, as long as we were locked down.

Day 30
24 April

Sunset's golden farewell
Glitters on roofs and trees,
Promising tomorrow's return.

Once again, nature came to my rescue, offering a stunning close to the day to remind me—remind us all—that there was beauty to be found, in spite of the pandemic.

Day 31
25 April

In the midst of the horror of a global pandemic came our commemoration of the horror of war. Anzac Day was even more quiet and reflective than usual. It was impossible not to compare the sacrifices we were being asked to make with those the soldiers in WWI made. By comparison, we sacrificed little and gained much.

Day 32
26 April

Level four was beginning to chafe, and kids and adults alike were going a bit crazy. Everyone was walking—sometimes three or four times a day—just to be doing something away from home.

Day 33
27 April

> Hush! Hush!
> The pines implore,
> But wind whips hissing past.
>
> We're late! We're late!
> The breeze insists.
> That's why we go so fast.

It seemed the wind was the only thing going anywhere. At least the weather was treating us to an extended summer. Warm weather and sunny skies allowed us to enjoy the outdoors.

Day 34
28 April

We moved to alert level three, but for most people little changed. Non-essential items were now available, but the shops that sold them were still closed. We ordered things online and eagerly awaited contactless delivery. A few students went back to school, but their learning was still delivered remotely, just as it was for the majority who remained at home. I continued my poems, because level three felt a lot like level four.

Day 35
29 April

Though alert level three didn't give us our normal jobs and school back, it did give us freedom to hop in the car and go somewhere (though not too far from home). My family enjoyed hiking in the mountains for the first time in weeks.

Day 36
30 April

The weather smiles
On our lockdown,
Offering us day upon day
Of glorious sun
Perfect for long walks,
A blue sky backdrop
For bike rides,
And warmth
For autumn crops.

We could grumble about the restrictions placed on us, but we couldn't complain about the weather Mother Nature provided. We felt blessed, in spite of everything.

Day 37
1 May

> The weekdays come,
> The weekdays go.
> Remind me again of the date?
> There's plenty to do
> And enough time to do it,
> But lockdown brain makes me late.

We'd survived all 1000 days of April, and we were desperately trying to find 'normal'. We were officially working and studying from home, but even so, the days slipped by with little feeling of accomplishment.

Day 38
2 May

Spider creeps across
A leaf nodding in the breeze,
Observed
    By a child cut loose
    From classroom walls.
Ten eyes
    Glitter
    With discovery.
Behold
    The great hunter
    Of your backyard.
    Student no longer
    But explorer of worlds.

I watched my students from afar. Some engaged in remote learning as if it were a video game. Others ignored our digital offerings, preferring instead to take full advantage of their freedom to make world around them their classroom.

There once was a mother locked in
with three kids and a dog. What
a din!
While her boss watched on Zoom
The kids pranced round the room
Wearing nothing but trash from
the bin.

I was fortunate to be stuck in lockdown with a sensible and studious teenager, but with three people trying to work and study in a shed, it was inevitable we'd bomb each other's Zoom meetings. Other parents struggled to work at all around homeschooling young children, and many resorted to locked doors and written schedules in order to work from home.

Day 40
4 May

Isolation was biting hard, but every day brought people to the fence to read my poems, and everyone was still striving to connect and be cheerful in the face of our collective struggles. In our solitude, we continued to reach out and connect with others however we could.

Day 41
5 May

Counting down the days and
 weeks,
Counting all the cases.
Keeping our distance, washing
 our hands,
Covering up our faces.
We listen to the daily briefing,
Hoping for the best.
For 'til we have the virus beat
We know we cannot rest.

For the second day in a row we had no new Covid-19 cases in New Zealand. We were holding our breath, crossing our fingers, not daring to hope we'd seen the last of the virus here.

Day 42
6 May

Dark clouds scour the sky.
Wind slices icicles through clothes,
And rain turns earth to mud.
We are dull and grey as the sky.
Confined.
Wondering when we can go out.

But storms pass.
Sun returns.
Saturated earth solidifies once again.
Days sparkle more brightly
Against a dark backdrop.

As we dreamt of the possibility of greater freedom in days to come, even simple pleasures like walking into a shop seemed like luxuries to be savoured.

Day 43
7 May

The government revealed what alert level two would look like, but not when we'd move there. The prospect of returning to workplaces, schools, and shops was both exciting and frightening.

A couple, their girl and a cat,
United, they all agreed that
Forty-four days
Blended into a haze,
And the boredom was
    making them fat.

The prospect of future freedom didn't alter the fact that the present confinement was turning all our brains to mush. We were more than ready to get out.

Day 45
9 May

We contemplated how life had changed, how we had changed during lockdown. The reality of the future was uncertain, but the natural world around us acted as an anchor.

Day 46
10 May

Alone
Still, empty
Worrying, fearing, frowning
Walls, restriction, creativity, freedom
Planning, connecting, laughing
Bustling, full
Together

It was sometimes difficult to reconcile our feelings of hope with the news from overseas, where the virus ran rampant. The end of our solitude was near, yet others remained in isolation with no end in sight. I felt a profound sense of survivor's guilt.

Day 47
11 May

With new Covid-19 cases trickling in, we knew there was still a risk the virus would flare up again. The move to level two loomed, and we planned for the increased vigilance it would require.

Day 48
12 May

On the penultimate day of lockdown, I reflected that everyone's lockdown experience was different. Everyone would have a different lockdown story. We would each remember different things about our collective experience. I decided to remember the aroha evident throughout New Zealand as we worked together while living apart.

> And so we come
> To the last lockdown poem.
> My thanks to the neighbours.
> I really do owe 'em
> For putting up with
> A host of bad rhymes
> And terrible verse
> A couple of times.
>
> The poems are done,
> But please don't be shy
> Introduce yourselves
> As you're walking by.

It was bittersweet to write the final pandemic poem. On the one hand, I felt my creative well was dry after so many days. On the other hand, I knew I would miss the challenge and I would miss listening to visitors read my poems and laugh.

I hope, as our lives return to a more normal routine, we can all hold onto the positive things we gained during lockdown. A sense of community, a greater appreciation for the natural world around us, a closer understanding of our bubble mates' needs, extra family time, shared walks ...

Kia kaha! Be well. Stay safe. Wash your hands.

About the Author

When I'm not scrawling bad poetry onto discarded building materials, I can be found writing speculative fiction for children and adults, or writing about food and the natural world on my blog.

Visit my website to discover all my books and other writing.

https://RobinneWeiss.com

www.ingramcontent.com/pod-product-compliance
Lightning Source LLC
Chambersburg PA
CBHW032256070726
47590CB00016B/3034